Lady Gaga

By United Library

https://campsite.bio/unitedlibrary

Table of Contents

Disclaimer

This biography book is a work of nonfiction based on the public life of a famous person. The author has used publicly available information to create this work. While the author has thoroughly researched the subject and attempted to depict it accurately, it is not meant to be an exhaustive study of the subject. The views expressed in this book are those of the author alone and do not necessarily reflect those of any organization associated with the subject. This book should not be taken as an endorsement, legal advice, or any other form of professional advice. This book was written for entertainment purposes only.

Introduction

The book Lady Gaga takes readers on a captivating journey through the extraordinary life of Stefani Joanne Angelina Germanotta, known worldwide as Lady Gaga. Renowned for her avant-garde style, innovative music and versatile performances, Lady Gaga has left an indelible mark on the entertainment industry.

Beginning her artistic journey as a teenager performing at open mic nights, Lady Gaga's determination and talent have taken her to the pinnacle of musical success. From her rise with hit singles "Just Dance" and "Poker Face" to the exploration of electronic rock and techno-pop in "Born This Way", the book navigates the evolution of her music. It explores her collaborations with Tony Bennett, her achievements as an actress and the monumental success of "A Star Is Born", making her the first woman to win major awards in music and film simultaneously.

The story explores Lady Gaga's resilience, image reinventions and impact on pop culture. With five consecutive albums topping the US Billboard 200, 13 Grammy Awards and numerous other honors, Lady Gaga's influence extends beyond music to comedy, fashion and philanthropy. This comprehensive biography offers a nuanced portrait of an artist who continues to push boundaries and inspire millions around the world.

Lady Gaga

Stefani Germanotta, also known as Lady Gaga (the song *Radio Ga Ga* is the origin of this pseudonym), born on March 28, 1986 in the borough of Manhattan, New York, is an American singer-songwriter and actress.

She got her start in the Lower East Side rock music scene, before making a name for herself with her debut album, *The Fame* (2008), which was a huge commercial success worldwide, with the number-one hits *Just Dance* and *Poker Face*. Her second album, *The Fame Monster* (2009), received rave reviews. This was followed by an eighteen-month world tour, *The Monster Ball Tour*, which became one of the most lucrative shows of all time.

With her third and fourth albums, *Born This Way* (2011) and *Artpop* (2013), she again reached the top of most charts, and topped the *Forbes* 2013 list of most influential musicians. She enters the world of jazz, recording two duo albums with Tony Bennett. Her fifth studio album, *Joanne,* marks a musical turning point for the singer, moving from country to pop-rock.

As an actress, Lady Gaga first played small roles in several TV series and films, before taking on larger roles in seasons 5 and 6 of the horrific anthology series *American Horror Story*. She then took on the lead role of Ally

Campana in the musical *A Star is Born*, which became a worldwide hit and whose soundtrack made Lady Gaga the artist with the most albums to reach number one in the US charts in the decade of 2010, while also winning her the Oscar for Best Original Song for *Shallow*. In 2021, she was again noticed for her role as Patrizia Reggiani in Ridley Scott's *House of Gucci*, and succeeded Margot Robbie as Harley Quinn in the musical thriller *Joker: Folie à deux*, scheduled for release in 2024. In 2022, she was named International Female Artist of the Year, one of the winners of the NRJ Music Awards 2022.

She is renowned for her eccentricities, performances and music videos. Her worldwide record sales in 2014 are estimated at 200 million, with 30 million albums and nearly 170 million singles according to *Billboard*. Awards include 13 Grammy Awards and 18 MTV Video Music Awards. She was named "Artist of the Year" in 2010 by *Billboard* magazine, has repeatedly appeared in various lists published by *Forbes* and was named "World's Most Influential Person" by *Time* magazine.

Biography

Childhood and beginnings

Stefani Joanne Angelina Germanotta was born on March 28, 1986, at Lenox Hill Hospital in New York, into an affluent family with a working-class background. Her father, Joseph, is the son of Italian immigrants and an Internet entrepreneur. Her mother, Cynthia, is of Italian-Scottish descent and a telecommunications assistant before becoming a stay-at-home mom. She has a younger sister, Natali, born in 1992.

At the age of 4, she began to learn the piano by herself and by ear, under the guidance of her mother. At eleven, she tried to get into Manhattan's Juilliard School, but changed her mind, and ended up at the Convent of the Sacred Heart, a private Catholic school.

She wrote her first ballads at the age of thirteen, and began singing on open stages, notably in jazz bars, when she was fourteen. She also won a jazz singing competition during this period. Admitted to high school, Stefani began to suffer frequent bullying at school because of her atypical physical appearance, prompting her to use her passion for art as a means of escape. Many of the songs she later wrote, such as Born This Way, encouraged her fans not to live for others, but to accept themselves as they were. In her first year of high school, she joined a rock band called "Mackin Pulsifer", which covered songs by Led Zeppelin, Pink Floyd and Jefferson Airplane. At the same time, she joined a jazz band and took part in school plays, playing the lead roles of Adelaide in *Guys and Dolls* and Philia in *A Funny Thing Happened on the Way to the Forum*. She then landed a small role in the Telltale Moozadell episode of The Sopranos. She then began to study the techniques of the famous "method acting" at the Lee Strasberg Theatre and Film Institute, and continued to do so for almost 10 years. She also studied the techniques of renowned theater practitioners Sanford Meisner and Stella Adler at their respective studios, while training in theatrical workshops at the Circle in the Square Theatre School.

At the age of 17, after auditioning, she was one of only twenty students in the world prematurely admitted to the renowned Tisch School of the Arts at New York University in Greenwich Village. She lived in dormitories, studied music and improved her style by writing essays on subjects such as art, religion and the socio-political order, including a thesis on photographer Spencer Tunick and artist Damien Hirst. Despite the fact that her school's rules forbade it, Gaga held auditions in parallel with her studies. She came very close to being selected to play Maureen Johnson in the American performances of the musical Rent, but was ultimately judged too young for the role. During this period, Stefani took part in her college's annual "Ultra Violet Live" musical competition, finishing third. She later managed to appear on an episode of *MTV's Boiling Points*, a prank show on the famous American music channel.

After leaving university to concentrate on her musical career, the very young woman began working in strip bars in New York, where she supplemented her income by working as a waitress. She was also a waitress at the Cornelia Street Café during this period, holding down three jobs, before briefly becoming a go-go dancer to make ends meet. She launches a *StefaniMusic website* and Myspace page to promote her career and connect with her early fans.

Difficult first steps (2005-2007)

Stefani Germanotta signed with Def Jam Records when she was just nineteen, after label boss Antonio Reid heard her singing in the hallway. Reid told her she was "a celebrity", and had her sign a contract on the spot. But once the contract had been signed, the young woman said she never saw him again, declaring that she "used to wait outside his office for hours, hoping he'd come and meet her and listen to her songs, but that never happened". Three meetings were scheduled between Reid and Stefani, but they were cancelled one after the other, before the label abruptly terminated the contract after three months, leaving the singer "upset". Def Jam Records wanted to keep the tracks Stefani had made after parting company with her, but she gave up part of the advance paid to her by the label in order to recover the rights to her songs. Among the tracks "recovered" by Stefani are Beautiful Dirty Rich and one of her future hits, Paparazzi.

Looking to bounce back after this setback, she began performing on the Lower East Side rock scene with the *Mackin Pulsifer* and *Stefani Germanotta Band,* also known as the *SGBand*, who produced an EP (mini-album) that was sold at their concerts. She also did solo shows at this time, opening for the rock band Nada Surf. At the same time, she began performing burlesque shows and taking cocaine. In October 2005, SGBand were invited to sing at the Columbus Day Parade in New York, and their performance was broadcast live on NBC's Channel 4. The band then performed frequently at *Mercury, St.Jerome's Lounge* and *The Bitter End*. It was at The Bitter End that Stefani Germanotta was spotted by author Maura Casey, who invited her to work on the writing and arrangement of the album accompanying the children's book *Scott and The Secret Dimension*. The young woman then had "an audience of fifteen to twenty people following her at every show", according to the band's guitarist, Calvin Pia.

The singer auditioned unsuccessfully for plays and musicals; pop music labels would not take her on, deeming her persona "too theatrical" for their taste. It was during this period, when she was 19, that she was raped by a music producer 20 years her senior. SGBand was subsequently chosen by Bob Leone, National Projects Director of the renowned Songwriters Hall of Fame, to be one of nine acts in the 2006 New Songwriters Showcase, a show designed to reveal new songwriters. During this show, the young artist was spotted by Wendy Starland, a collaborator of music producer Rob Fusari, who had previously worked with Will Smith and Destiny's Child. Starland strongly recommended that Fusari collaborate with the young singer-songwriter, and Fusari listened to her songs on the Internet before inviting her into the studio. He compared her vocal style to that of Freddie Mercury, quickly giving her the nickname Gaga, inspired by the song *Radio Ga Ga* by Mercury's band Queen. She then began using her current stage name: Lady Gaga.

In 2007, Gaga collaborated with Lady Starlight, who helped her create her stage universe. The duo began performing in clubs on the Lower East Side, with Gaga designing and sewing her stage outfits. The concerts are called *Lady Gaga and the Starlight Revue*, billed as the ultimate burlesque show in tribute to 1970s variety. In August of the same year, Gaga and Starlight were selected to perform at the Lollapalooza *American Music*

Festival in Chicago. The show was very well received and received good reviews. Around this time, Gaga also opened for the independent glam-rock band Semi Precious Weapons in front of 400 people in New York.

Having initially focused on avant-garde and electro dance music, Gaga found her niche when she began to incorporate pop into her melodies and vintage glam rock à la Bowie or Queen into her mix.

She then signed a songwriting contract with Akon's Konvict Muzik label, creating songs for Fergie, the Pussycat Dolls, Tamy Chynn, Nicole Scherzinger, Britney Spears and New Kids on the Block. After hearing her sing a *vocal guide* (a recording of a song by a third party to guide its final performer) for one of his tracks, Akon decided that she was also a talented singer. This prompted him to convince Interscope Records president Jimmy Iovine to sign a joint deal with his own label. Thanks to her new affiliation with Akon, she began work on her debut album, produced by RedOne.

Already possessing a number of electro-glam tracks à la David Bowie or Queen, she decided to mix her retro dance beat with urban melodies and a pop chorus, while retaining a rock and roll edge. The first song she produced was *Boys Boys Boys*, inspired by *Girls, Girls, Girls* (from the album of the same name) by glam metal band Mötley Crüe and the song *T.N.T.* (from the album of the same name) by hard rock band AC/DC.Before the release of her album, *The Fame*, she declared that her "goal as an artist is to write and make pop music that has something artistic and interesting to say. If I can reach a four-year-old girl as well as a 25-year-old art student with my album, then I'll have done a good job."

The Fame and The Fame Monster (2008-2010)

At the beginning of 2008, Gaga moved to Los Angeles, where she worked with her record company to perfect her album *The Fame*. She then set up a creative collective called Haus of Gaga to create her outfits, sets and sounds. It was at this point that she met another young singer, Lina Morgana, who became a close friend and with whom she co-wrote -many songs that were never marketed. Lina died tragically at the age of nineteen in mysterious circumstances. This surprising death, and Lady Gaga's failure to comment on it, gave rise to far-fetched conspiracy theories. The collaboration between the two women gave rise to twelve songs that were illegally uploaded to the web during the early days of the Internet.

Some radio stations found Gaga's music too "dance-oriented", too "80s" or "too daring" for the general public at the time, and refused to play it, but the singer persevered until her career finally took off with the release of the track *Just Dance*, featuring the vocal participation of Colby O'Donis. The song reached number

1 in many countries, including Canada, the Netherlands, Ireland and the UK, but took almost a year to break through in the United States. Over four million copies of the single are sold in less than five months. A promotional single, *Beautiful, Dirty, Rich, was* released shortly after *Just Dance.* The album, *The Fame*, was released in October 2008, selling over twelve million copies. This was followed by *Poker Face*, which went straight to No. 2 in France (week of January 26-February 1, 2009) and No. 1 (week of February 23-March 1). This single was number 1 in every country where it was released. In 2009, *Poker Face was the* best-selling song in the world, with almost 10 million copies sold. The third single chosen is *LoveGame*. Promotion of Gaga's first opus ends with the singles *Eh, Eh (Nothing Else I Can Say)* and *Paparazzi*.

Lady Gaga declares, in an interview with *Métro Québec*: "A year from now, we'll be meeting in this very pub, people will still be talking about me, and even better, I'll be more famous than ever!" Lady Gaga first appeared on television at the Miss Universe 2008 contest, where she performed *Just Dance*. She then appeared on Fox's *So You Think You Can Dance. Later,* the song *Beautiful, Dirty, Rich* was used in the promotional video for the ABC series *Dirty Sexy Money.*

On July 4, 2008, blogger Perez Hilton organized a concert for Lady Gaga at a private nightclub in Los Angeles; the influential king of the "web jet set" described her live performances as "extremely innovative". Nominated for the 2008 MTV Video Music Awards in the categories of "Best Newcomer of the Year" and "Best Music Video", she didn't win any awards, declaring herself content with her success in the charts. During this period, Gaga goes on tour with her *The Fame Ball Tour*.

On March 29, 2009, Gaga was invited to sing with a contestant at a variety show on Quebec's *Star Académie*, with Ginette Reno and Roger Hodgson. In April 2009, she becomes the first artist since 1999 to have her first two singles debut at #1 on the Billboard 100. At the end of May 2009, Hilton, who calls her "the new princess of pop", previews the sixth video clip from *The Fame* album, *Paparazzi*, on his blog.On July 13, 2009, *Billboard* magazine reported that Gaga was the third artist in the history of the *Mainstream Top 40* to have three No. 1 singles from a debut album, after Mariah Carey's debut album and its five No. 1 singles, *Ace of Base* in 1993-1994, Christina Aguilera in 1999-2000 with her debut album *Christina Aguilera* and three No. 1 singles, Avril Lavigne in 2002-2003 with her album *Let Go* and her three No. 1 hits. Investing a lot of money in her shows, Gaga is now bankrupt for the fourth time since the recent launch of her career.

On November 18, 2009, Gaga's second album was released. Entitled *The Fame Monster, it is a* reissue of the singer's first opus, with eight additional tracks. The album also features an edition in which the tracks from *The Fame do not* appear. *The Fame Monster is both* a reissue of Gaga's first opus and an album in its own right.

The album is marketed under two different covers: the first shows Gaga wearing a blonde wig and a leather jacket. The second shows her wearing a long black wig and weeping blood of the same color. The album was released in all countries on November 23, 2009, with the exception of Japan, where it was released on November 18, 2009, and Australia and Germany on November 20, 2009. The singer claims that she began writing *The Fame Monster* during her first tour (*The Fame Ball Tour).*

The first of the four singles, *Bad Romance, was* officially released in the U.S. on October 26, 2009. The track is a commercial success, and its video becomes the most viewed in Youtube history. The second single, *Telephone, features a* collaboration with singer Beyoncé Knowles. *Telephone* was originally written for Britney Spears, but after she turned it down, the song was used on Lady Gaga's album. *Telephone* was released on January 26, 2010 in the U.S. and April 6, 2010 in France. The third single, Alejandro, unveiled via Twitter, was released on April 20, 2010 in the United States. The fourth single and first promotional single from the album is *Dance in the Dark*. The track was not released in the U.S., nor was it accompanied by a video clip.

To promote her album, Gaga made a number of TV appearances, including one on Barbara Walters, one on Ellen DeGeneres, one on the *X Factor* talent show, and an appearance on the drama series *Gossip Girl* (season 3, episode 10). Lady Gaga was also invited to the *Royal Variety Show*, alongside Miley Cyrus, to perform one of her songs for Queen Elizabeth II. She performed *Speechless* on a piano almost three meters high. To promote *The Fame Monster,* she also created a world tour visiting four continents: *The Monster Ball Tour. The Fame Monster is* awarded an Australian platinum disc at the end of December, its first certification. At one point, the tour lost $3 million after the singer refused to compromise on the staging, but eventually became the most lucrative artist tour in history. Shortly afterwards, the album received its second certification, an American Gold Record. By the end of the year, the album had become the second best-selling album of 2009, behind Susan Boyle, beating Lady Gaga by just 100,000 sales.

In early 2010, she teamed up with electronics brand Polaroid, and presented a model of her *Herbeats* headphones at the *Consumer Electronic Show*. In mid-January, she performed *Monster, Bad Romance* and

Speechless on the Oprah Winfrey show. There, she announced that all proceeds from her New York concert on January 24 would be donated to a charity for earthquake survivors in Haiti. In the end, Lady Gaga managed to raise half a million dollars, or three hundred thousand euros. For the biggest musical event of the year, the *Grammy Awards,* she performs *Poker Face*, dressed in a shiny green outfit, in its original version, and sings *Speechless* and *Your Song* with Elton John. A few days after the *Grammy Awards*, Gaga declares in an interview for 102.7 KIIS-FM radio that she has started work on her third album, and that the video for *Telephone* will be a sequel to the one illustrating her hit *Paparazzi*. At the Brit Awards, Gaga sings *Dance in the Dark* and an acoustic version of *Telephone*. Her performance was a tribute to American fashion designer Alexander McQueen. She wins each of the three categories in which she is nominated.

In mid-March, Fusari, her former producer, lodged a complaint against her, claiming $30.5 million, claiming that he had co-written *Paparazzi* and *Beautiful, Dirty, Rich*, and that he had only received $600,000, less than the 15% of the profits from these two songs that he should initially have received. He also stated that it was he who introduced Gaga to Interscope Records and came up with her stage name. The singer and Mermaid Music LLC filed a counterclaim, settling the legal issues and closing the case after the complaints were dropped. The singer's grandfather, Giuseppe Germanotta, died of Parkinson's disease in September 2010.

Born this Way and *ARTPOP* (2011-2014)

While receiving the Best Video of the Year award for *Bad Romance* at the *2010 MTV Music Awards*, Gaga sang a short extract from the theme song of her forthcoming album, *Born This Way*. The single was written in 10 minutes by the singerShe subsequently posted the single's release dates on Twitter on New Year's Day. In the end, the track was released two days early. The song is a worldwide success, reaching number 1 in 19 countries. On April 15, 2011, she releases the second single from the album, *Judas*. Two weeks before the album's release, she unveils the single *The Edge of Glory*, inspired by the death of her grandfather. Finally, a week before the album's release, she releases the first and last promotional single: *Hair*. The choice of the fourth single to promote the album is made official later in the year: it will be *Yoü and I*. On August 16, 2011, the video was leaked, forcing Gaga to release it three days ahead of schedule. *Marry the Night* is the fifth single from the album. A short extract from the video was unveiled on November 17, 2011: it was released in its entirety on December 2, and is the singer's longest clip. During an appearance on *Taratata* in France, she announced that she would like to release nine or ten singles from the same album, a project that ultimately came to nothing.

Released on May 23, 2011, the album comes in two editions: the standard edition, which includes fourteen tracks, and the deluxe edition, which contains seventeen tracks plus six remixed songs, making a total of twenty-three tracks.

At the *MTV Video Music Awards,* Gaga appeared on the red carpet dressed as Jo Calderone, her male alter ego. She opened the ceremony with a speech, followed by a performance by *Yoü and I,* accompanied by Queen guitarist Brian May. During the evening, she receives two awards for her *Born This Way* video.

At the end of the year, the bestsellers of the year are revealed. Gaga's *Born This Way* album took second place worldwide, selling more than 2.1 million copies in the U.S. and over 5.5 million worldwide. Since then, the album has sold over eight million copies. There's another surprise in the chart, with *The Fame Monster coming in at* number twenty-two. In terms of singles, *Born This Way* is number six, while *The Edge of Glory is number* sixteen. There are rumors of *Heavy Metal Lover* as the sixth single, but *Born This Way*'s run may end with *Marry The Night*. The rumors come to an end on March 22, 2012, with the official announcement that the *Born This Way album has been* discontinued, and that the singer has withdrawn from the media spotlight. The song *Scheiße* is then used to promote her new perfume Fame. Shortly afterwards, she begins her world tour *The Born This Way Ball*, on April 27, 2012 in Seoul, South Korea.

On June 27, 2012, at one of her concerts in Melbourne, Australia, she presented the public with a brand new piece of music: *Princess Die*. This new track shocked some of her audience with its reference to Princess Diana, including the line "I want to drive away in my rich lover's limousine, right after he proposes with a sixteen-carat diamond wrapped in rose gold, with the paparazzi swarming all around. So put your head down for another dead blonde". Australians, many of whom come from families of former English settlers, don't appreciate the singer's indelicate treatment of the princess story. For the first time on tour, she alludes to her new album. She confides, however, that she does not yet know whether or not this unreleased music will be part of her fourth album, due in 2013. Gaga breaks her hip on stage, forcing her to end her tour prematurely and spend some time in a wheelchair. In 2012, Gaga opens her own social network for fans, LittleMonster.com. Gaga appears in the 2013 edition of the Guinness Book of Records as "the world's most famous personality". On October 9, 2012, she accepted in person the peace prize named "*The LennonOno Grant for Peace*" awarded by Yoko Ono.

On December 25, 2012, Gaga announced via her social network, as well as on Twitter, that Terry Richardson was working on a documentary about Gaga's life, the *Haus of Gaga* and the creation of the singer's new opus. Gaga then announces the album title and her preference for it to be stylized in capital letters, resulting in *ARTPOP*.

New songs for her fourth studio album, *ARTPOP*, were completed while she was working with producer Fernando Garibay in early 2012. In a May 2012 interview, the singer's manager, Vincent Herbert, announced that she had already begun work on the project during her *Born This Way Ball*. The singer's label considered that the finished album contained no future hits and tried to alter its content, but the star wished to leave the album as it had been conceived.

The album was released on November 11, 2013, and immediately received rather mixed reviews. However, it becomes her second album to reach number one on the US Billboard 200 chart, selling 258,000 copies in its first week. This result is still lower than the launch of her previous album *Born This Way* in 2011, but the first two singles taken from it are well received: *Applause* and *Do What U Want*. *The album's* third and final official single, *G.U.Y.,* failed to chart, but the promotional single *Dope made it into the* top 10.

During this period, the singer suffered a breakdown as a result of her difficulties in coping with the chronic pain from which she had been suffering for a year and a half, as well as the betrayals of several friends and members of her team, and the comments of certain media who already saw her career as buried. The album continues to be poorly promoted, with a number of up-and-coming singles being dropped, as well as the video clips for *Do What U Want* and *Venus*.

The singer made her grand return to the stage on August 25, 2013 at the *MTV Video Music Awards* with a performance, retracing every facet of the singer, on her single *Applause*. She also opens the iTunes Festival in September 2013, during which eight songs from the new album are performed. During the album launch party in Brooklyn, Gaga shows off a *Haus of Gaga* creation: *Volantis*, the first flying dress. The singer is also a presenter on the November 16 episode of *Saturday Night Live*, closing the program with a performance alongside Kelly. At the American Music Awards, she also sings *Do What U Want* with Kelly. Later in the month, she appears in a Thanksgiving special, "Lady Gaga and the Muppets' Holiday Spectacular" alongside the Muppets, Elton John, Joseph Gordon-Levitt and RuPaul.

Having wanted to act in a film from an early age, the singer made her film debut with a role in Robert

Rodriguez's *Machete Kills*. She plays the role of *La Chameleón*. The action film hit cinema screens on October 4, 2013. Gaga then appeared in the film *Sin City: I Killed for Her*, by the same director, released on August 22, 2014. She also became the face of Italian haute-couture brand Versace in early 2014 for the "Lady Gaga for Versace" campaign. In September 2014, she released her second fragrance in association with Coty, *Eau de Gaga*.Gaga played the final concerts at the *Roseland Ballroom*, New York and then embarked on a world tour a few months later named *ArtRave: The Artpop Ball*. The latter raked in a total of $83 million across 79 dates worldwide. Meanwhile, the singer parted ways with her manager, Troy Carter following "artistic differences" and in June 2014, she and her new manager, Bobby Campbell, joined *Artist Nation*, the management division of Live Nation Entertainment. Her worldwide record sales in 2014 are estimated at 180 million, 30 million albums and almost 150 million singles according to *Billboard*.

Cheek to Cheek, American Horror Story, Joanne, the Super Bowl and Enigma (2014-2017)

In 2014, Gaga and American jazz artist Tony Bennett released a collaborative album called *Cheek to Cheek*, in which they covered jazz standards together. The two singles from the album, *Anything Goes and I Can't Give*

You Anything But Love, both debut at the top of the US jazz singles chart.

The album, meanwhile, was released on September 19, 2014 in France and then on September 24 in the rest of the world. It debuts at #1 on the Billboard 200 with 131,000 copies sold in its first week. The album receives many positive reviews and earns Bennett and Gaga a Grammy Award in the "Best Traditional Pop Vocal Album" category at the 57 annual *Grammy Awards* ceremony on February 8, 2015. Together they embark on a world tour, the *Cheek to Cheek Tour*, visiting a dozen countries across 36 dates. On December 22, 2014, Gaga confided to Yahoo! that she had already started work on her new album. In January 2015, RedOne and producer Giorgio Moroder confirmed their involvement in writing the opus. At the 87th Academy Awards on February 22, 2015, the singer gives an extremely well-received performance of a medley from the film *The Sound of Music*. She also performed John Lennon's *Imagine at the* opening ceremony of the first edition of the *European Games* in Baku on June 12, 2015.

Gaga also writes a song with Diane Warren, for the documentary *The Hunting Ground*, entitled *Til It Happens To You*. The song is nominated for a Satellite Award and an Oscar. In June, Gaga receives the first Contempory Icon Award at the 46th *Songwriters Hall of Fame*. She performed a cover of *What's Up?* by 4 Non Blondes. *Forbes* ranks the singer as the 25th highest-paid celebrity between June 2014 and June 2015, with total earnings of $59 million. Gaga is also voted "2015 Woman of the Year" by *Billboard.* In October of the same year, the singer appeared in a video for Tom Ford's Spring 2016 campaign in which she covered Nile Rodgers' *I Want Your Love* accompanied by models. That same day, she became the first artist to have two singles sell more than 7 million copies in the United States.

In February 2015, Gaga confirmed her appearance in season 5 of the TV series *American Horror Story,* entitled *Hotel.* She lends her features to Countess Elizabeth Johnson, a hotel owner and the season's main character. Her role in the series earned her the Golden Globe for Best Actress in a Miniseries or TV Movie during the 2016 ceremony. The singer confided to *Entertainment Weekly* magazine that her experience as an actress in the series greatly influenced the writing of the opus. In March 2016, Gaga confirmed her appearance in the sixth season of *American Horror Story, Roanoke,* scheduled for September 2016. She plays a Celtic witch named Scáthach, appearing in just a few episodes.

In January 2016, Gaga was invited to edit the 99 issue of *V* magazine, which featured sixteen covers. The singer is named Editor of the Year at the *Fashion Los Angeles*

Awards for her work. On February 7, she sings the American national anthem for the 50th *Super Bowl* game. Gaga also pays tribute to David Bowie at the *Grammy Awards* in a collaborative performance with Intel and Nile Rodgers. At the 88th Academy Awards, she performs her song *Til It Happens To You*, accompanied by 50 victims of sexual assault. Her performance is introduced by U.S. Vice-President Joe Biden.

On August 17, 2016, Gaga announced via Instagram and her website the release of her new single *Perfect Illusion*. A promotional single follows, *A-YO*, as well as the second single, *Million Reasons*. To promote the forthcoming release of her album, Gaga undertakes a short three-date tour, the *Dive Bar Tour*. A final tour in July is added. On September 15, she announced that her new album would be called *Joanne*, in tribute to her father's sister, who died at a young age from Lupus. Released on October 21 of the same year, the album reached number one in the U.S. charts and the top 10 in many countries around the world. On September 30, after lengthy discussions, she announced on her Twitter account that she would be performing the 51 *Super Bowl* half-time show, taking over from Coldplay. The show becomes the most-watched musical performance of all time. On April 16, 2017, Gaga, who is one of the headliners at the Coachella festival, performs her new single, *The Cure, for the* very first time. The track is immediately available on digital download platforms and reaches number one on Itunes in over 60 countries. In June, it was announced that the singer would soon be unveiling new tracks.

In August 2017, the singer embarked on an international *Joanne World* Tour. In September of the same year, a documentary focusing on the singer was unveiled exclusively on Netflix, entitled *Gaga: Five Foot Two*. In it, Gaga reveals that she has been suffering from fibromyalgia for several years, and declares that she is taking a break from her musical career. Her poor health forced Gaga to postpone the European dates of the *Joanne World Tour* until 2018. Even with a whole series of dates postponed until the following year, the tour became the most lucrative by a female artist in 2017.

After numerous rumors, the singer confirmed on December 19, 2017 that she would begin a residential tour, dubbed *Lady Gaga Enigma*, in Las Vegas the same month of the following year, from 30 to 80 dates depending on the media with a record fee that would exceed $1 million per concert.

A Star Is Born, Chromatica (2018-2020)

In October 2018, the film *A Star is Born*, a remake of the Hollywood classic, was released, directed by Bradley Cooper, who also stars as the male lead. Gaga plays the lead role of Ally and also composed the film's soundtrack.

Her performance received critical acclaim at screenings at the Venice Film Festival and the Toronto International Film Festival. The film and its soundtrack subsequently met with immense critical and commercial success. The soundtrack even reached the top 10 best-selling albums worldwide in 2018, despite being released at the end of the year. Lady Gaga is nominated for an Oscar for Best Actress and, on February 24, 2019, wins for Best Original Song (for *Shallow*). The track goes on to reach number one on the US charts, and is the song by a female artist that spends the longest time at number one on the Itunes World chart, ahead of Adele's *Hello.* The album sold 6 million copies 8 months after its release, becoming the third best-selling album of 2019 in the United States and reaching 8 million copies sold in 2021.

In July 2019, Gaga makes official the creation of her first cosmetics brand *Haus Laboratories*. Launched on Amazon, the brand immediately tops the sales charts in the beauty products section.

In February 2020, the singer announced the release of a new single, *Stupid Love*, which reached number five on the US sales charts. She then announces the release of a house-sounding album entitled *Chromatica* for April 10, 2020. However, on March 24, the singer announced the postponement of her album, to a later date in 2020, due to the coronavirus pandemic. On May 22, Gaga unveils the single *Rain on Me*, in collaboration with singer Ariana Grande, which reaches number one in the U.S. charts. The album, which proved to be a return to Gaga's pop and dance roots, was released on May 29 and reached the top of the charts in France, England, Italy, the United States and Canada, among other countries. In September, Gaga becomes the face of Valentino's *Viva Voce* perfume, which uses her song *Sine from above* in its video advertising, while *911* becomes *Chromatica*'s third single, accompanied by a short film clip by Tarsem Singh.

On November 20, 2020, she announced on social networks that she would be attending the "Lupus Research Alliance", where she would virtually perform her song Joanne (song), from her fifth album of the same name Joanne (album), in tribute to her aunt who died of the disease.

On December 2, 2020, she announces on social networks, that the promotion of her sixth album Chromatica resumes, the star decides to unveil her collaboration with the famous brand Oreo, with which, she decides to create new cookies in the colors of her album, which will be marketed in limited edition worldwide from January 2021. She also announced that five new remixes of her hit *911* would be released in early December, in addition to her new edition of Chromatica. At the same time, the star make-up brand *Hauslabs* achieves sales of $141 million for the year 2020, just one year after its launch.

On January 20, 2021, she sings the American anthem at the inauguration ceremony of the 46th President of the United States of America, Joe Biden. In February 2021, she begins shooting House of Gucci, Ridley Scott's new film. However, shortly before she began shooting her new film in Italy, her dog walker Ryan Fischer was hospitalized after being shot in Hollywood. Two of her French bulldogs, Koji and Gustav, were taken away while a third dog named Miss Asia escaped and was later recovered by police. Gaga then offered a $500,000 reward for the return of her pets. Two days later, on February 26, a woman brought the dogs to a police station in Los Angeles. Both were unharmed. Police said the woman who dropped off the dogs did not appear to be involved in the shooting. On April 29, LAPD said five people had been charged with the robbery, including the woman who had returned the pets. On March 31, 2021, Lady Gaga unveiled her collaboration with champagne house Dom Pérignon, to be released on April 6. A promotional clip is produced featuring *Free woman*, Lady Gaga's new French single. At the Brit Awards 2021, Rina Sawayama revealed that she was taking part in the Chromatica remix album.

For a time, she was considered for a female role in the action film *Bullet Train*, alongside Brad Pitt, but eventually withdrew due to scheduling conflicts, and Sandra Bullock took her place.

Cinematic turn with *House of Gucci* and *Joker 2* (since 2022)

Lady Gaga continues her cinematic ascent by starring in the crime drama *House of Gucci,* directed by Ridley Scott. The film centers on the murder of Maurizio Gucci, son of the founder of the Italian luxury brand, by his ex-wife Patrizia Reggiani, played by Gaga. The role enabled her to star alongside such prestigious actors as Al Pacino, Jeremy Irons, Adam Driver, Jared Leto and Camille Cottin. For her performance, Gaga relies on the actors studio technique. For almost two years, she took Italian lessons to perfect her accent, turned brunette and read numerous biographies. The biopic becomes the highest-grossing dramatic film in theaters since 2019, confirming its success thereafter. However, it does not receive the support of the main character concerned, Patrizia Reggiani criticizing her counterpart's performance and the film in general. The critics were on the whole rather cold, but praised Lady Gaga's performance. The artist picked up her 5th Golden Globe nomination, this time in the Best Actress in a Motion Picture Drama category.

She then took part in the development of the soundtrack for the action film *Top Gun: Maverick*, the sequel to the 1986 phenomenon, alongside composers Lorne Balfe,

Harold Faltermeyer and the multi award-winning Hans Zimmer. Her contribution included the song *Hold my hand.* The film was a huge success, grossing 1.454 billion at the international box-office and receiving excellent reviews from audiences and press alike. *Hold My Hand* was also nominated for an Oscar 2023 and a Golden Globe for Best Original Song.

In August 2022, she landed the coveted role of Harley Quinn in the sequel to the psychological drama *Joker* entitled *Joker: Folie à deux* . The film turns out to be a new horror-tinged musical. She succeeds Australian actress Margot Robbie, who has played the role in three films: *Birds of Prey* in 2020 and both parts of *The Suicide Squad* in 2021. The latter is very supportive of the artist, appreciating the fact that two actresses share the same role at the same time, but in different projects. Shooting of the film alongside Joaquin Phoenix is scheduled to finish in April 2023.

In April 2023, she was appointed Chair of the *President's Committee on the Arts and Humanities* by U.S. President Joe Biden.

Privacy policy

In a 2009 interview, she revealed her bisexuality. Her song *Poker Face* makes reference to this, telling the story of a woman thinking of another woman during sex with her partner.

Between 2005 and 2008, she dated Luc Carl, a DJ and nightclub owner. She then briefly dated music producer Rob Fusari from November 2008 to February 2009, and an entrepreneur nicknamed Speedy - whom she met on the set of the *LoveGame* video - from March to July 2009. She also had an affair with stylist Matthew "Dada" Williams, from September 2009 to January 2010.

Gaga got back together with Luc Carl in July 2010 and got engaged to him the following October. However, they separated again in May 2011. In July 2011, she became the girlfriend of actor and model Taylor Kinney, whom she has known since the filming of the *Yoü and I* video. In February 2015, she announced their engagement, but on July 19, 2016, she announced that they had decided to take a break from their relationship. She became a couple with actors' agent Christian Carino in 2017 and got engaged to him before they separated in 2019. The singer briefly entered into a relationship with sound engineer Dan Horton in the summer of 2019. That same year, at a party organized by her friends, Lady Gaga met Michael Polansky, an engineer and manager of a philanthropic foundation who has been her companion ever since.

Over the years, she has revealed that she suffered from depressive episodes from a very young age, and explains that her mental health deteriorated after she was repeatedly raped at the age of 19. She explains that she went through phases of self-mutilation and claims to be undergoing medical and therapeutic treatment to combat the post-traumatic stress disorder and depression with which she has been diagnosed.

She also suffers from fibromyalgia, a disease that causes chronic pain throughout the body, associated with fatigue, cognitive problems and sleep disorders, and she says she uses transcendental meditation to relieve her pain.

Lady Gaga is godmother to Elton John and David Furnish's two sons.

Influences, fashion and public image

Gaga has been influenced by rock and glam rock musicians such as David Bowie and Freddie Mercury, Pink Floyd, Led Zeppelin, Iron Maiden, Black Sabbath and Bruce Springsteen, as well as pop icons like Britney Spears, Grace Jones, Madonna, Cyndi Lauper, Prince, Cher, Mariah Carey, Liza Minnelli and Michael Jackson.

The song *Radio Ga Ga is the* source of her pseudonym; she says: "I loved Freddie Mercury and his band Queen, they called one of their songs *Radio Ga Ga*. It was a unique song, just like Freddie, who was one of the greatest pop personalities.

She frequently cited fashion icon, actress and singer Grace Jones as an inspiration.

Madonna, who first met Gaga at the *2009 Video Music Awards*, claimed in an interview with *Rolling Stone magazine* that she found a part of herself in Gaga. Following comparisons between Madonna and herself, Gaga declared, "I don't want to sound modest, but I aim to revolutionize pop. In my opinion, the last revolution was launched 25 years ago by Madonna".

She is also often compared to singer Debbie Harry from the band Blondie. In the June 2, 2010 edition of an article in the online music magazine *Side-Line*, she states that she has recently become a fan of the English band Erasure, whose lead singer she met at a DJ show in the summer of 2009, as well as Depeche Mode. Andy Warhol is repeatedly portrayed by Gaga as an important influence.

Gaga herself has declared that fashion is "everything" to her. She frequently collaborates with Nicola Formichetti, once artistic director of haute couture house Thierry Mugler. She considers Italian Donatella Versace to be her main fashion inspiration, along with designer Jan Klod, and also cites Isabella Blow. In 2012, Gaga wore the iconic say *that* dress by Gianni Versace, and in 2014 she was the Italian brand's publicity image, photographed by Mert and Marcus. The previous year, she walked the runway for Thierry Mugler. In summer 2015, she appeared in an advertisement for the Tom Ford brand. In 2016, she repeated the catwalk experience, this time for a Marc Jacobs collection. The Tudor watch brand chose her as its ambassador in 2017. She also made her mark by wearing to the 91 Oscars a Tiffany&Co necklace (of which she is the image) made legendary by Audrey Hepburn at the release of the American film classic *Breakfast At Tiffany's*. In 2020, Valentino announced that she would be the face of its *Viva Voce* fragrance. In April 2021, the star became the new ambassador for French champagne house Dom Pérignon.

Her love of fashion stems from the fact that, as she says, "when I write music, I think about the clothes I'd like to wear on stage or just on the street. Fashion is everything; art, performance and pop. Fashion comes with a lot of other things, things that will get me really good fans. I want them to want to eat me and lick every part of me because my clothes are so striking. The *Global Language Monitor* named Gaga one of the most special fashion icons on the planet.

She has her own production team called *Haus of Gaga*, although she personally takes care of the gadgets and some of her outfits. The team creates many of Gaga's clothes, theatrical accessories and wigs. Among other things, the *Haus of Gaga* created the famous Disco Sticks that the singer has been using since her *LoveGame* video. In July 2019, the singer who has previously been the face of Shiseido or MAC announces the launch of her own cosmetics brand "Haus Laboratories" on Amazon exclusively.

Gaga calls her fans Little Monsters. She had "Little Monster" inscribed on her left arm as a tribute to them in January 2010. She has 23 other tattoos, including a symbol of peace and love inspired by John Lennon, who, according to *The Guardian*, was Lady Gaga's hero, a quotation from the poet Rainer Maria Rilke on her arm and a symbol of unity between victims of sexual assault on her back.

Gaga has the range of a contralto. Her voice has been compared to that of Gwen Stefani, while the structure of her music is inspired by 1980s pop and 1990s europop. As for her lyrics, journalist Sarah Rodman for *The Boston Globe* writes that "her lyrics make you dance without even trying". Simon Reynolds, for his part, asserted that "Lady Gaga's style is mainly Electroclash, except for a few songs that have a 1980s, pop and R&B feel".

She is frequently regarded as a gay icon.

Philanthropy and positions

In addition to her musical career, Gaga has been involved with a large number of charities (non-profit, in a personal capacity) throughout her career. The causes she supports include access to education, the fight against poverty, child protection, gender equality around the world, assistance for people living with disabilities, job placement assistance, LGBT rights, the fight against cancer, support for victims of harassment, help for the homeless, preservation of the environment, the fight against sexual violence, access to healthcare and hygiene products/services, relief for victims of natural disasters and fires, the fight against AIDS as well as support for HIV-positive people and access to sex education, help for people suffering from addiction, access to protective equipment for nursing staff, the fight against food insecurity, access to sport, support for communities affected by mass shootings, the fight against human trafficking, support for victims of domestic violence and sexual assault, the fight against hunger, the regulation of firearms ownership in the United States, support for people recovering from addiction to one or more substances, assistance for the elderly, support for schools, aid for medical research, access to and support for culture, the fight against fibromyalgia, help for victims of mental illness, support for the children of incarcerated people, freedom of expression and freedom of information.

In October 2009, Gaga and many other celebrities auctioned cards they had signed to raise funds for the fight against Alzheimer's disease.

In February 2010, Gaga took part in the AMFAR Gala to raise funds for the fight against AIDS.

Following the earthquake in Haiti in 2010, she gave a concert with all proceeds going to help rebuild the country. The concert took place on January 24, 2010. On the same day, proceeds from sales of merchandising products on Gaga's official online store bolstered the campaign. The total amount raised was 500,000 US dollars, or 350,000 euros.

Gaga is also committed to educating young people about the risks of HIV. In collaboration with Cyndi Lauper, she teamed up with the M.A.C. Foundation, a cosmetics manufacturer, which raised over $160 million for this common cause. To this end, they launched their *Viva Glam Gaga* and *Viva Glam Cindy lipstick* lines. All proceeds were donated to M.A.C. in support of HIV-infected people. In a press release, Gaga says: "We want women to feel strong, strong enough to remember that they need to protect themselves. Our aim is for this lipstick to act as a kind of reminder. When your man is naked in bed and you go to the bathroom, put on your lipstick and take a condom with you. There shouldn't be any exceptions...". In an interview with *Marie Claire* magazine, Gaga asserts that "she didn't join the solidarity campaign just to create a lipstick, but to help people". In January 2010, the singer promoted Beats' *new Monster RED Special Edition* headphones in Las Vegas, with $5 from every sale going to support AIDS programs in Africa that provide testing, counseling, treatment and other services for AIDS sufferers.

To continue promoting safe sex, the star is designing and promoting a line of condoms for the Proper Attire brand. All profits will go to Planned Parenthood.

In May 2010, the singer took part in a charity concert to raise funds for the fight against deforestation, alongside Sting, Bruce Springsteen and Elton John.

In June 2010, Gaga sang at the *White Tie & Tiara Ball*, a fundraising gala for the Elton John AIDS Foundation.

That same year, Gaga auctioned off 4 VIP Tickets/ Meet & Greet Passes for her concerts to raise funds for *The Young Storytellers Foundation*, which teaches writing, literature and self-confidence free of charge in inner-city schools in Los Angeles.

Gaga offers PREMIUM VIP tickets for her concerts to fans who have donated their time to associations helping homeless youth. This gesture generates 30,000 hours of voluntary public service for hundreds of associations across the United States. For each date of her Monster Ball Tour, Gaga donates $20,000 to associations helping homeless LGBT people. Gaga takes part in a video in which she encourages her fans to donate to Virgin Mobile's *RE*Generation* campaign in support of homeless youth. The singer pledges to match donations made to this campaign up to a total of $25,000.

Gaga auctions off a Steinway piano signed by her to benefit Ten O'Clock Classic. This charity provides weekly music lessons and instruments to New York City elementary schools on a volunteer basis, as well as free performances and classes in schools across the United States. It also auctions VIP tickets for the charity Project ETHE.

In November 2010, Gaga visited the *Royal Children's* Hospital in Australia to fulfill the wish of a child who had asked her to join the *Starlight* charity.

That same month, Gaga took a break from social networking to motivate her fans to raise a million dollars to fund AIDS treatments for people without access to them in Africa and India.

In the aftermath of the March 2011 earthquake in Japan, Gaga rallied to the aid of the victims, creating the design and phrase "*We pray for Japan*" on red and white plastic bracelets - the colors of the Japanese flag - to be ordered online. Gaga announced via Twitter at the end of March that the bracelets had earned the country almost $1.5 million (around €1.03 million). In June 2011, Gaga's various actions to help earthquake victims raised three million dollars for the cause.

In April 2011, Gaga donated $1 million to five associations fighting poverty and helping the homeless.

In May 2011, Gaga performed at a Gala organized by the Robin Hood association, which assists children and adults living with disabilities.

That same month, Gaga publicly opposed the immigration reform law passed in Arizona and declared that she had written her song *Americano* in protest against the law.

Also in May 2011, the star donated part of the profits from the country version of her hit *Born this way* to the GLSEN association, which fights bullying of LGBT young people in schools.

In March 2011, Gaga donated $1.5 million to the Japanese branch of children's rights organization Save the Children. In June 2011, Gaga takes part in MTV Video Music Aid Japan, with proceeds donated to the Japanese Red Cross.

In 2012, Gaga donated $1 million to the New York Red Cross for the victims of Hurricane Sandy.

Gaga is a very active supporter of LGBT rights around the world. Having committed herself to changing local legislation in the USA, she has repeatedly campaigned to influence the policies of Barack Obama and Donald Trump on this issue. She supports same-sex marriage and same-sex parenting, publishing a video urging people in 4 US states proposing same-sex marriage in referendums to vote in favor. She also took a public stand for the repeal of the *Don't Ask, Don't Tell law* with a public speech, a video urging US citizens to contact their local senator about the possible repeal of the law and by bringing with her soldiers discharged from the army because of the VMA carpet law in 2010 to raise awareness of the cause. In 2011, she met with Obama to discuss ways of combating harassment, particularly homophobic harassment, in schools. She will cancel her agreement to sell an unreleased version of her *Born This Way* album with the Target supermarket chain, which has publicly supported groups opposed to gay rights. The singer offered to return to the original agreement in exchange for donations from the company to LGBT associations, but the retailer refused, and Gaga definitively abandoned any plans for collaboration. In May 2011, she took part in the *It Gets Better* operation in support of LGBT youth. In 2016, she visited the Ali Forney Center (en), an association that helps LGBT street youth, and brought gifts to young people helped by the association. In 2018, she publicly opposed Donald Trump's exclusion of trans people from the military. That same year, the Trump administration considered abolishing federal recognition for trans people, and Gaga publicly criticized the project on several occasions. She is also considered a "gay icon".

In March 2012, Gaga launched her *Born This Way Foundation* association with her mother to help young victims of bullying and to combat the malaise and depression affecting some teenagers. The association makes mental health professionals available free of charge during the journeys of its *Born Brave Bus*. In two years, the bus has seen over 150,000 visitors. The organization also offers mental health first aid training throughout the United States.

In August 2012, Gaga and other celebrities joined Yoko Ono and Sean Lennon's "Artist against fracking" initiative opposing the controversial technique of hydraulic fracturing.

In September 2012, Gaga once again supported *The Young Storytellers* association. She launched a contest to meet her, with the special feature that participants had to make a donation to the association in order to be entered.

In October 2012, Gaga won the *Lennon Ono Grant For Peace Award*. The singer chose to donate it to the *Elton John Foundation* to help "orphans or disadvantaged youth in the United States born with the AIDS virus or AIDS".

In November and December 2012, Gaga made two humanitarian trips as an ambassador for Unicef to Peru and South Africa. During her trip to Peru, the singer spent Thanksgiving with 45 young girls who had been sexually abused, and gave them food at the *Caritas Felices* center in Lima, which fights poverty.

That same year, Gaga declared herself in favor of abortion and the legalization of cannabis.

In January 2013, she took part in a charity dinner organized by the *Chicago Bulls* basketball team to benefit associations supporting education, the health and well-being of young people, the fight against violence and support for the military and first responders.

In August 2013, Gaga took part in the *Hands for marriage equality* concert in support of the legalization of gay marriage in Atlantic City.

In October 2013, Gaga took part in a video produced as part of a fundraiser for a Hudson museum.

That same year, Gaga auctioned off tickets for her shows to raise money for the children's charity *Children United USA* and the charity *SportsSpectacular*, which funds diabetes research, healthcare planning to avoid or minimize the risk of disease in children, and research into the development of cutting-edge trauma care methods.

In January 2014, Gaga auctioned off 2 VIP tickets for her concerts, as well as a meeting with her, on the specialist charity auction site *Charitybuzz*. This action was done to benefit the victims of the Sandy Hook Elementary School mass shooting, the second largest mass killing by a single person in U.S. history. She's doing it again this time to help the *Arms around children* association, which provides safe homes for vulnerable orphaned children at risk of being exploited, infected or affected by AIDS, rescued from human trafficking, abused or living without adults in India, Ghana and South Africa.

In May 2014, Gaga visited the *Gilette children's* Hospital in the city of Saint Paul as part of the "No pity visit" campaign to raise awareness of the cause of disabled children.

In July 2014, Gaga joined the "Save Our Water" campaign to combat the advanced drought affecting the state of California.

In December 2014, Gaga auctioned off objects to support the MusiCares association, which supports musicians in difficulty by offering emergency financial aid, recovery programs for people suffering from addiction and social assistance.

In March 2015, Gaga took part in the *Polar Plunge* to raise money for the *Special Olympics* sports organization, which aims to train children and adults with intellectual disabilities in sport, as well as organizing sports competitions for them. She took part in the *Polar Plunge for the Special Olympics again* the following year.

That same month, she took part in the *"One smile"* operation to raise funds for children born with malformations in developing countries where access to reconstructive surgery is limited, and made a personal donation. She will repeat the experience the following year.

In July 2015, Gaga bought $295,000 worth of goods at a charity auction organized to assist the victims of the Nepal earthquake.

That same month, Gaga co-hosted a gala with Tony Benett, with proceeds going to the WellChild (en) charity,

which supports sick children and their families across the
UK.

In August 2015, Gaga and some thirty politicians,
celebrities, activists and bosses signed an open letter to
raise awareness of women's rights around the world.

In October 2015, Gaga took part in the Amfarde Los
Angeles Galal to raise funds for AIDS research.

In January 2016, Gaga co-wrote and performed a song
about sexual assault for the documentary *The Hunting
Ground (en)* tackling sexual violence on American
campuses. She will also raise awareness of the issue
during a public discussion after the film's screening. This
intervention will also be published on the internet

In February 2016, Gaga participated for the second time
in the GRAMMY Foundation auction, dedicating items
sold to help the MusiCares organization.

In March 2016, Gaga published a series of posters on her
social networks to raise awareness of sexual assault in the
workplace.

That same month, Gaga took part in the World Water Day
campaign, aimed at alerting the world to the risks of
future water shortages.

In April 2016, Gaga participated in the launch and
fundraising of the *Parker institute for cancer*

immunotherapy aimed at supporting cancer research creating 6 oncology research centers.

In June 2016, Gaga and the Dalai Lama promoted the *City of Kindness* initiative, aimed at encouraging mayors to commit to "compassionate projects" such as youth mentoring programs, support for the homeless, community beautification and clean-up, support for the dependent, help for senior citizens, as well as multiple other forms of volunteerism aimed at citizen self-help and the public interest. In August 2016, Gaga joined US Vice President Joe Biden on his tour of American colleges for the *It's on Us* campaign. The initiative aims to break the taboo of sexual assault on student campuses as well as inform students of existing resources for any victims of sexual assault. During the 2016 US presidential election, Gaga supported candidate Hillary Clinton, who lost to Donald Trump. The singer, who declares she "has nothing to say about him", is known to dislike the politician. She therefore demonstrated and campaigned several hours after Trump's victory.

On June 23, 2016, Gaga and other celebrities sign an open letter published in Bilboard Magazine calling on the U.S. Congress to require background checks for all gun purchases and ban anyone on the "terrorist watch list" from buying a gun. On June 29, Gaga takes part in a Human Rights Campaign video made in response to the shooting at the *Pulse* gay club in Orlando. The video aims to encourage US citizens to ask their political representatives for stricter legislation on the prevention of gun violence, as well as on the protection of LGBT people from discriminatory attacks against them.

In July 2016, Gaga lent her support to Black Lives Matter, an activist movement fighting racial discrimination.

In February 2017, Gaga again offered autographed items at the GRAMMY foundation's annual charity auction in aid of the MusiCares association.

In August 2017, Gaga made a financial donation to Louisiana flood relief.

In April 2017, Gaga signed a guitar put up for auction to raise funds for Planned Parenthood of America. In May 2017, Gaga publicly lent her support to whistleblower Julian Assange by taking part in a film defending him. The film features a meeting between the man under house arrest and the singer who visited him. In June 2017, Gaga launched a fundraiser to help schools pay for supplies.

In June 2017, Gaga collaborated with coffee chain Starbucks to launch *Cup of kindness.* This collection of drinks aims to raise funds for support for people with mental health problems.

In October 2017, she publicly criticized the political world's lack of action to counter gun violence.

Since autumn 2017, Gaga has frequently used her celebrity to raise awareness of the causes and consequences of Fibromyalgia.

Lady Gaga donates $1 million to support the victims of the hurricanes that hit the United States and the Caribbean. She later took part in a benefit concert for the cause.

In December 2017, the singer's association *Born this Way Foundation* donates all its donations received from December 19 to the following January 19 to some 30 local associations supporting foster youth, the LGBT community, the children of incarcerated people or giving school meals 5 days a week to young people from working-class families at greatly reduced prices, among others.

In May 2018, Gaga decided to expand her foundation by having the title *Channel Kindness* trademarked. This new branch of the association aims to provide food and furniture for people in need and their children, childcare services for the children of teenage mothers, temporary accommodation for them and their children, meals for destitute people leaving hospital, give financial assistance to individuals and local associations who show compassion in their initiatives, services and activities for people in need as well as helping and organizing fundraisers to encourage inter-university sports competitions among others.

That same month, Gaga once again took part in the GRAMMY Foundation auction, this time in aid of *Girls Rock Camp Alliance.* The organization offers summer camps and educational programs around the world, enabling young girls to learn to play instruments, compose and perform.

In June 2018, she took part in a fundraiser for the *Children mending heart* association, which fights against school bullying.

In October 2018, Gaga took part in the March For Our Lives demonstration to call for more oversight of gun ownership in the United States.

In November 2018, Gaga made a financial donation to the Red Cross after the violent fires that hit California and visited several shelters with food to comfort victims evacuated from their homes. She encourages her fans to do the same by donating or volunteering. The singer is publicly criticizing the Trump administration's lack of action in the face of the devastation caused by the fires. To encourage donations to help the victims, Gaga's foundation announced on November 13 that for every donation made by individuals to one of its partner associations, the foundation would donate an equal amount to that partner. Entitled the *MultiplyYourGood Challenge*, the campaign motivates potential participants by offering a draw to attend a Gaga show in Las Vegas for anyone who takes part in the challenge, and promotes it on social networks to encourage further donations.

That same month, Gaga collaborated with Bono and the RED organization to raise money for the fight against AIDS. The association organized a lottery in which each voucher was given in exchange for a donation to RED, and the two artists created a song specifically for the winner, dedicating the original booklet containing the lyrics.

In December 2018, Gaga created stickers in collaboration with Swarovski aimed at raising funds for the British Fashion Council's *Education Foundation*. Profits are used to financially support fashion students.

In May 2019, Gaga will take part for the fourth time in the Metropolitan Museum of Art's annual ball to raise funds for the museum's *Costume Institute*.

In June 2019, Gaga authorized the use of several songs she co-wrote and performed for the film A Star Is Born as part of an *A Star is Born This Way* show, with a portion of the proceeds going to the Born This Way foundation.

In August 2019, Gaga announced that she would fund school projects in 162 classrooms in cities that had suffered mass killings between Texas, California and Ohio via her Born This Way Foundation.

In September 2019, actress Indya Moore revealed that Gaga had, in 2013, made "a very generous donation" to the foster care agency that was then taking in her and other orphaned minors.

On February 1, 2020, the singer's foundation collaborated with AT&T TV, which donated $250,000 in exchange for the star's concert for the brand's Super Bowl festival.

In April 2020, Gaga made a donation to the *Americas Food* Fund to distribute meals following the economic hardship caused by the Covid-19 crisis. *Hauslab*, the star's cosmetics brand, donates 20% of its earnings for one week to support food banks in New York and Los Angeles following the food insecurity created by school closures. The singer also worked with the humanitarian organization *Global Citizen* to raise funds, and personally contacted 70 business leaders and philanthropists, raising $35 million to equip medical staff, improve the speed of tests, help find a vaccine and treatments, and combat the economic consequences of the virus. Subsequently, she and the organization organized the Together at Home concert in support of healthcare professionals, featuring performances and messages from a host of celebrities including Elton John, Lizzo, Chris Martin, J. Balvin, Paul McCartney, Maluma, Billie Eilish, John Legend, The Rolling Stones, Beyoncé, David Beckham, Sam Smith, Céline Dion, Oprah Winfrey, Christine and the Queens, Andrea Bocelli, Jennifer Lopez, Michelle Obama, Stevie Wonder and herself. The eight-hour concert will be broadcast live on Youtube. Following the show, Gaga and *Global Citizen's* campaign raised a total of $127 million.

That same month, Gaga announced that for her upcoming *The chromatica ball* tour, one euro or dollar from every ticket sold would be donated to her foundation.

From May 29 to May 31, 2020, Lady Gaga has pledged to donate $1 to the *World Central Kitchen* association, which provides meals to the underprivileged, for every order placed on the Postmates website.

Also on May 31, Gaga once again denounced police violence and systemic racism in the United States, as well as Donald Trump's political action on these issues. On June 5, she made donations to several associations acting against these scourges, then let these same organizations address her millions of fans via her social network accounts.

On June 30, 2020, Gaga signed NIVA's tribune in support of independent venues during the Covid-19 pandemic asking Congress to release funds to support them.

On June 25, Gaga took part in a fundraising event for the *Marsha P Johnson Institute*, which defends the rights of black trans people.

It has been announced that the singer's foundation will now receive $1 from every transaction made to benefit her cosmetics brand.

On November 2, Gaga took part in a political meeting as part of Joe Biden's presidential campaign, where she denounced her political opponent Donald Trump's comments on women.

In January 2021, following the election of Joe Biden as President of the United States, Gaga, who had actively supported the Democratic candidate, was chosen by him to sing the American national anthem on the steps of the Capitol during the inauguration ceremony on January 20.

In April 2021, the singer recorded a video calling for more resources for psychological support for people living with HIV, which was shown at Elton John's Oscar pre-party.

That same month, the artist teamed up with champagne brand Dom Pérignon to release a limited series of sculptures she had painted and signed, with all proceeds going to the *Born This Way Foundation*.

In May 2021, Gaga took part in the documentary *The Me You Can't See,* aimed at raising public awareness of mental health issues.

In March 2022, the singer's foundation is offering online courses to help young people and those in contact with them to take care of their mental health and detect symptoms, as well as to better support sufferers.

In April 2022, Gaga's foundation is collaborating with the *Crunchy Rolls* brand to create a clothing collection to use the proceeds for her foundation.

In July 2022, the singer launched a line of eyewear in collaboration with *Pair eyewear*, with 20% of the profits going to her foundation.

In August 2022, the foundation began distributing donations to 22 youth support associations via its *Kindness in community* fund, which delivers a total of $1 million in donations.

Awards, tributes and impact

Lady Gaga has received a total of over five hundred awards and has been nominated over 750 times. The singer received thirteen Grammy Awards during her career. In May 2014 and December 2015 respectively, she won the RIAA Digital Diamond Awards for each of her hits *Poker Face* and *Bad Romance*, both of which are among the rare songs to have sold more than ten million copies in the USA. She is the first female artist to receive this award. She is also the first artist to break the billion-view barrier on YouTube, and was the most-searched person on the web between 2010 and 2011. She is second only to Oprah Winfrey in *Forbes'* "Most Powerful Celebrities of 2013" ranking, and was the artist with the most albums reaching number one on the US charts in the 2010 decade. She topped the *Forbes* 2013 ranking of most influential musicians ahead of Beyoncé, Madonna and Bon Jovi.

Lady Gaga is the artist with the most nominations in a single year at the VMA Awards, the biggest ceremony rewarding the best music videos of the year. She achieved this record by collecting 13 nominations for the 2010

ceremony, where she also became the most awarded
artist in one edition, with 8 wins that night. The video for
Bad Romance was voted "Best Video of the 21st Century"
by music magazine and music industry institution
Bilboard. In October, the singer's song *Poker Face* became
the most downloaded song in UK history, while her track
Just Dance came third.

In October 2010, the world's first Gaga exhibition, "Gaga à
Gogo", by Alexandra Boucherifi, was held at the Galerie
Chappe in Paris. In November of the same year, the singer
entered the Guinness Book of Records as the artist with
the most weeks in the British charts, beating the record
held by the English group Oasis.

In 2011, Gaga received the Fashion Icon award from the
Council of Fashion Designers of America.In 2013, Gaga
won two awards for her fragrance *Fame*: "Best Flagrance
for Women" at the Swedish Beauty & Cosmetics Awards
and People's Choice at the Canadian Fragrance Awards.
That same year, the singer's album The Fame was named
one of the "best debut albums of all time" by Rolling
Stones magazine.

In 2012, she was the subject of a temporary exhibition,
The Elevated. From the Pharaoh to Lady Gaga, marking
the 150th anniversary of the National Museum of
Warsaw.

In 2015, she won the Icon award at the Songwriters Hall of Fame, a prestigious institution that honors musical authors and composers. In January 2016, she received a Golden Globes Award for "Best Actress in a Miniseries" for her performance in *American Horror Story: Hotel*. In March 2016, Gaga was named "Editor of the Year" at the Fashion Los Angeles Awards for her work for V magazine.

In 2018 and 2019, Gaga's performance in A Star Is Born earned her back-to-back "Best Actress" awards at the Critics' Choice Movie Awards, then from the National Board of Review, the Dublin Film Critics' Circle as well as the Phoenix Film Critics Society. She was also nominated in the same category at the Oscars, Golden Globes and Satellite Awards. The song *Shallow* from the film wins *Best Song* at the 2019 Golden Globes, the Critics' Choice Movie Awards and the 91st Academy Awards, before being voted Song of the Decade at the GoldDerby Awards.

According to Kathleen Pryer, Professor of Biology at Duke University and Director of the Duke Herbarium, a species of American fern has been named *Gaga in* homage to the singer, an ardent defender of equality and individual expression. She points out the resemblance of a heart-shaped Armani stage costume worn by Lady Gaga to the gametophyte of a fern. What's more, the presence of the GAGA sequence in the DNA of this new fern species sets it apart from all the others. One of the species in this genus, discovered in Costa Rica, was named *Gaga Germanotta after the* artist's family. A species of grasshopper discovered in Nicaragua, the *Kaikaia Gaga*, was also named after the singer.

Lady Gaga is frequently regarded as an artist who has changed popular culture, pop music and fashion, as well as influencing the general public's perception of LGBT people.

She is also widely recognized as one of the artists who helped popularize Synthpop music in the late 2000s and early 2010s, when these tracks were initially only played in nightclubs and very rarely represented in mainstream media. She topped *Times* magazine's "Most Influential People of 2010" in the artist category, and was voted "Most Influential Artist" of 2011 by the prestigious *Forbes Magazine*. That same year, she was ranked seventh in *Forbes'* list of the world's most powerful women. Her influence continues to be recognized by many media observers.

His work has influenced artists such as Miley Cyrus, Cardi B, Nicki Minaj, Dua Lipa, Ava Max, Ellie Goulding, Halsey, Doja Cat, Justin Timberlake, Rina Sawayama, Nick Jonas, Beyoncé, Sam Smith, Jon Batiste, Kanye West, Noah Cyrus, SZA, Jennifer Lopez, Kesha, Katherine Langford, MGMT, Rachel Zegler.

In 2023, she was named co-chair of the Committee for the Arts and Humanities, an advisory commission whose role is to advise the White House on cultural policies.

© John Bauld

Controversy and media censorship

In 2009, the video for *LoveGame was* censored on Australian TV for its "frequent sexual references, both verbal and visual". In 2010, American Idol partially censored her performance of Alejandro, judging it too sensual for its viewers. In summer 2010, the singer wore a dress made of meat to the VMA Awards, which caused a stir around the world, particularly among animal rights groups. The singer explained on The Ellen DeGeneres Show that the concept was to show the public that everyone will end up being treated like "a piece of meat" if they don't fight for their rights. The star had come that evening to the red carpet of the VMA awards with US servicemen who were victims of the "Don't ask, don't tell" law, to support them in their quest for new rights, giving full meaning to the metaphor represented by this dress.

That same year, the video for his song Alejandro was deemed blasphemous by some, and relegated to the post-midnight slot on one of MTV's channels for its combination of erotic, religious, S&M and Nazi imagery. The clip's content choices will be explained to journalists as metaphors by its director Steven Klein. The use of religious vocabulary and iconography in some of the star's videos and songs (notably on the Born This Way album) caused scandal on numerous occasions. Malaysian radio stations partially censored the song *Born This Way* for its lyrics: "no matter gay, straight or bi, lesbian, transgender I'm on the right track".

In 2011, the song Judas caused a scandal because it contained the lyrics "Je suis amoureuse de Judas" ("I'm in love with Judas") and was released at Easter time. It was publicly condemned by Bill Donahue, president of the American Catholic League. In May 2011, the Fox television network censored the artist's shoes because they depicted erect penises.

That same year, Gaga saw several of her tracks censored on Chinese online music sites, as the government declared that they were "detrimental to the security of state culture".

In April 2012, an ironic tweet from the star about the restrictive aspect of her diet caused a scandal. Perceived by many as an apology for anorexia, it received widespread criticism from Internet users, as well as disapproval from the National Eating Disorders Association.In May 2012, Gaga was refused permission by the Indonesian national police to perform in Jakarta, despite the fact that tickets for the show had already sold out. Interior Minister Gamawan Fauzi later welcomed the decision. The Council of Ulemas, Indonesia's highest Islamic religious body, had previously lodged a complaint against the singer's visit to the country, recommending that she not be accepted. The Front for the Defense of Islam (FPI), known for its violent raids, had vowed to gather "thirty thousand" demonstrators in Jakarta to prevent the singer from "spreading her satanic faith". The president of the FPI, Habib Salim Alatas, described her to AFP as a "destroyer of faith", adding "Repens-toi Lady Gaga. Repent. You should wear an abaya (loose-fitting dress) and a veil and stop singing toxic songs". A protest involving several hundred conservative Korean Christians to cancel the star's Seoul concert had previously taken place to no avail. In the Philippines, hundreds of activists from the Christian group BibleMode Youth demonstrated to demand the cancellation of the star's concert in Manila.

Other Philippine organizations calling for the concert to be cancelled include The Intercessors for the Philippines, the Philippines for Jesus Movement, the Philippine Council of Evangelical Churches, Bible Mode Baptist Group, NFS Ministry, Metro Manila for Jesus Movement and Tribes and Nations Outreach. Manila Representative Benny Abante, who is also a religious leader, warns concert organizers and sponsors Smart Telecom, SM and Ovation Productions Inc that the religious groups will go to court if the concert goes ahead, and declares that the concert would be a violation of the country's Penal Code, which states that anyone who publicly exhibits or causes the exhibition of any indecent or immoral show that "offends race or religion" will be imprisoned from 6 months to 6 years, adding "I remind Lady Gaga that she does not have diplomatic immunity, unless she wants to stay here for 6 years". The mayor of Pasay City, part of the Manila suburbs, finally declared that the concert had to be adapted to the country's morals and issued a statement saying he had formed a group to monitor the event. The singer sang her song Judas during the show, despite requests from opponents. In September 2012, the singer stirred up the anti-cannabis community by smoking cannabis on stage during her Born This Way Ball tour.

In January 2013, Gaga incurred the wrath of anti-gun activists by wearing a "machine-gun bra" to her concerts after the Sandy Hook shooting tragedy. A few months later, Lady Gaga's song *Aura* caused controversy, with some seeing it as insulting to veiled women and others accusing her of promoting the veil. In 2013, the cover of the ARTPOP album was censored in China in favor of a revised version, less revealing than the original. The song Sexxx Dreams on the album is also renamed X Dreams. This is not the only place where the album cover is censored: the version sold in the Middle East is also modified, as are the covers of the singles Do What U Want and Dope.

In 2014, a performance by the artist in collaboration with Millie Brown caused controversy as it was accused of promoting eating disorders. The artist will defend her right to artistic expression by defending her choice of medium, in this case paintings made via vomiting matter. In May 2014, the singer saw her Artrave show censored in Dubai.

In 2016, Gaga was personally banned from China after her entire repertoire was banned from broadcast and download in the country. The decision came after the singer's meeting with the Dalai Lama, a highly contested figure in China.

Discography

Solo albums

- 2008: *The Fame*
- 2009: *The Fame Monster*
- 2011: *Born This Way*
- 2013: *Artpop*
- 2016 : *Joanne*
- 2020: *Chromatica*

Other

Collaborations

- 2014: *Cheek to Cheek* in collaboration with Tony Bennett.
- 2021 : *Love For Sale* in collaboration with Tony Bennett.

Original soundtracks

- 2011: *Gnoméo et Juliette* in collaboration with Elton John, Bernie Taupin

- 2018 : *A Star Is Born* in collaboration with Bradley Cooper, Mark Ronson...

- 2022: *Top Gun: Maverick* in collaboration with Hans Zimmer, Lorne Balfe...

Appearances on other albums

- 2008: *Video Phone* featuring Beyoncé (*I Am... Sasha Fierce*)

- 2008: *Big Girl Now* featuring New Kids on the Block (*The Block*)

- 2009: *Chillin'* featuring Wale (rapper) (*Attention Deficit*)

- 2011: *Hello Hello* featuring Elton John (*Gnoméo et Juliette*)

- 2011: *Lady is The Tramp* featuring Tony Bennett (*Duets II*)

- 2011: 3-Way (The Golden Rule) featuring The Lonely Island and Justin Timberlake (*The Wack Album*)

- 2018*: Your Song (Revamp: songs by Elton John and Bernie Taupin*)

- 2018: *I Want Your Love* featuring Nile Rodgers and Chic (band) (*It's About Time*)

- 2023: *Gimme Shelter* featuring the Rolling Stones in concert in 2012 (*GRRR Live!*)

- 2023: *Sweet Sounds of Heaven* featuring the Rolling Stones and Stevie Wonder (*Hackney Diamonds*)

Tours

Solo

- 2009: *The Fame Ball Tour*

- 2009-2011: *The Monster Ball Tour*

- 2012-2013: *The Born This Way Ball*

- 2014: *ArtRave: The Artpop Ball*

- 2017-2018 : *Joanne World Tour*

- 2022: *The Chromatica Ball*

Residences

- 2014 : *Live At Roseland Ballroom*

- 2018-2020: *Enigma*

- 2019-2022: Jazz & Piano

In collaboration with

- 2014-2015: *Cheek To Cheek Tour*

Promotional

- 2016: *The Dive Bar Tour*

Filmography

Executive Producer

- 2011: Judas (song)

- 2011: Lady Gaga Presents: The Monster Ball Tour at Madison Square Garden

- 2011: Yoü and I

- 2011: A Very Gaga Thanksgiving

- 2013: Applause (song)

- 2013 : Lady Gaga & the Muppets' Holiday Spectacular

- 2014: Tony Bennett & Lady Gaga: Cheek to Cheek LIVE!

- 2016 : Perfect Illusion

- 2016: Million Reasons

- 2017: Gaga: Five Foot Two

- 2018 : Lady Gaga: Joanne - Piano Version

Director

- 2011: Lady Gaga: Google Chrome

- 2011: Lady Gaga: Marry the Night (Clip)

- 2011: A Very Gaga Thanksgiving (TV show)

- 2014 : Lady Gaga: G.U.Y. (Clip)

Year 2010

- 2011: *Gnoméo et Juliette* by Kelly Asbury - writing of the song "Hello, hello" with Elton John

- 2012: *Men in Black 3* by Barry Sonnenfeld: herself (cameo)

- 2013: *Machete Kills* by Robert Rodriguez: The Chameleon (3 transformations)

- 2014: *Operation Muppets* (*Muppets Most Wanted*) by James Bobin: herself (cameo)

- 2014: *Sin City: J'ai tué pour elle* (*Sin City: A Dame to Kill For*) by Robert Rodriguez: Bertha, the waitress

- 2018 : Bradley Cooper's *A Star Is Born*: Ally Campana-Main (also co-composer of the songs)

2020s

- 2021: *House of Gucci* by Ridley Scott: Patrizia Reggiani

- 2022: *Top Gun: Maverick* by Joseph Kosinski - (co-composer and performer of the song *Hold my Hand)*

- 2024: *Joker: Folie à deux* by Todd Phillips: Harley Quinn - (also co-composer of the songs)

Documentaries

- 2012: *Katy Perry, the film: Part of Me* (*Katy Perry: Part of Me*) by Dan Cutforth and Jane Lipsitz (cameo)

- 2012: *The Zen of Bennett* by Unjoo Moon

- 2015: *Jeremy Scott: The People's Designer* by Vlad Yudin

- 2021: *The Me You Can't See*

TV series

- 2001: *The Sopranos*: a young girl (season 3, episode 9)

- 2009: *Gossip Girl*: herself (season 3, episode 10)

- 2012: *The Simpsons*: herself (voice - season 23, episode 22)

- 2015 : *American Horror Story: Hotel*: Countess Elizabeth Johnson

- 2016 : *American Horror Story: Roanoke*: Scáthach (3 episodes)

- 2021: *Friends: The Reunion*: herself (guest)

Documentaries and *Special*

- 2011: *Gaga by Gaultier* by Alex Fighter and Julie Gali

- 2011: *Lady Gaga Presents the Monster Ball Tour: At Madison Square Garden* by Laurieann Gibson

- 2011: *Lady Gaga: Inside the Outside* by Davi Russo

- 2011: *A Very Gaga Thanksgiving* by herself

- 2013: *Who The F-k is Arthur Fogel* by Ron Chapman

- 2013 *: Lady Gaga and the Muppets' Holiday Spectacular* by Gregg Gelfand

- 2014: *Tony Bennett and Lady Gaga: Cheek to Cheek Live!* by David Horn

- 2017: *Gaga: Five Foot Two* by Chris Moukarbel

- 2019: *How To Be: Mark Ronson* by Carl Hindmarch

- 2021: One Last Time: An Evening with Tony Bennett and Lady Gaga by Alex Coletti

Special events

- 2015: Performance of the American national anthem during the Superbowl half-time show.

- 2017: Superbowl half-time show

- 2021: Performance of the American national anthem, The Star-Spangled Banner, at the inauguration of President Joe Biden.

TV Juror

- 2011: *American Idol*: Guest mentor (May 11, 2011 show)

- 2011: *So You Think You Can Dance*: Guest judge (broadcast July 28, 2011)

- 2017: *RuPaul's Drag Race*: Guest judge (broadcast March 24, 2017)

Fragrances

- 2012: *Fame* The fragrance achieved the best start (first-week sales) in fragrance history behind Chanel's *Coco,* and became the best-selling fragrance of 2012 in the UK.

- 2014: *Eau de Gaga*

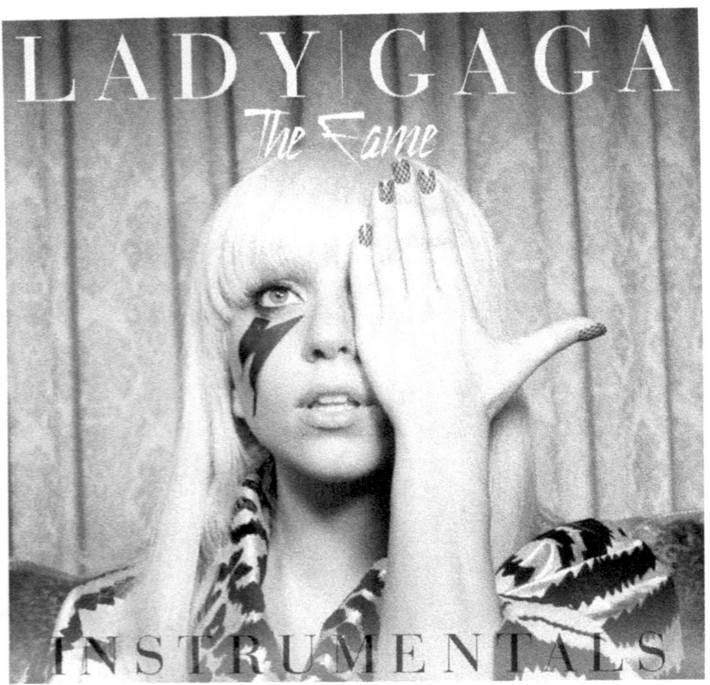

LADY GAGA
The Fame
INSTRUMENTALS

Other books by United Library

https://campsite.bio/unitedlibrary

www.ingramcontent.com/pod-product-compliance
Lightning Source LLC
Chambersburg PA
CBHW080353030625
27637CB00014B/869